JAPAN

Ali Brownlie

Photographs by Masanori Kobayashi

CHERRYTREE BOOKS

Distributed in the United States by
Cherrytree Books
1980 Lookout Drive
North Mankato, MN 56001

Library of Congress Cataloging-in-Publication Data
Brownlie, Alison, 1949-
   Japan / by Ali Brownlie.
     p.cm. -- (Letters from around the world)
   Includes index.
   ISBN 1-84234-256-8 (alk. paper)
   13-digit ISBN (from 1 January 2007) 978-1-84234-256-5
   1. Children--Japan--Social life and customs--Pictorial
works--Juvenile literature. 2. Japan--Social life and
customs--1945--Pictorial works--Juvenile literature. I.
Kobayashi, Masanori. II. Title. III. Series.

DS822.5.B75 2004
952.05 22
                                2004041448

First Edition
9 8 7 6 5 4 3 2 1

First published by
Evans Brothers Ltd
2A Portman Mansions
Chiltern Street
London W1U 6NR

Conceived and produced by

Nutshell
MEDIA

www.nutshellmedialtd.co.uk

Editor: Katie Orchard
Design: Mayer Media Ltd
Cartography: Encompass Graphics Ltd
Artwork: Mayer Media Ltd
Consultants: Jeff Stanfield and Anne Spiring

© Copyright Evans Brothers Limited 2003

All photographs were taken by Masanori Kobayashi.

Printed in China.

Acknowledgments
The author and photographer would like to thank the
following for their help: the Kobayashi family, and the
teachers and students at Fumi's school in Osaka.

Cover: Fumi and his baseball friends.
Title page: Fumi winds up on the mound.
This page: Mount Fuji — Japan's highest mountain.
Contents page: Fumi and his brother Sota ski in the
   mountains in Nagano.
Glossary: Fumi washes the windows from the balcony.
Further information page: Fumi's friend practices
   writing Japanese characters on the chalkboard.
Index: Laying down a bunt in a baseball game.

Contents

My Country

Saturday, January 5

7-1-14-564
Kitamidorigaoka
Osaka 560-0001
Japan

Dear Nicky,

Ossu! (This is how we say "hi" in Japanese.)

My name is Fumi Kobayashi and I'm 9 years old. I live with my family in Osaka, a big city in Japan. I have a brother, Sota, who's 11, and a sister, Maya, who's 14. I'm really excited about being your penpal. I hope we can learn a lot about each other.

Write back soon!

From
Fumi

Here I am (in the middle) standing on a wall outside a Buddhist temple with Mom, Dad, Sota, and Maya. ➞

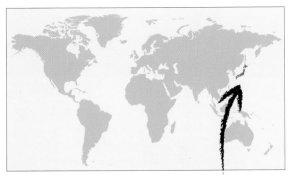

Japan's place in the world.

N

PACIFIC OCEAN

Hokkaido
Sapporo

JAPAN

Sea of Japan

0   100   200   300   400 kilometers

0   100   200 miles

Shinano

JAPANESE ALPS

Honshu

Nagano

Tone

Kawasaki   TOKYO

Kyoto   Nagoya

Hiroshima   Kobe   Yokohama
Osaka   Mount Fuji
12,385 ft
(3,776 m)

Shikoku

Kyushu

East China Sea

PACIFIC OCEAN

Japan is made up of a chain of nearly 4,000 islands. Most people live on the four big islands of Honshu, Hokkaido, Shikoku, and Kyushu.

This map shows the four main islands of Japan. Osaka is on Honshu.

Osaka is Japan's third-largest city. It has a population of 2.5 million. Osaka is more than a thousand years old, but today it is a busy modern city with towering office buildings.

This is Midosuji, the main road of Osaka, which connects the north to the south.

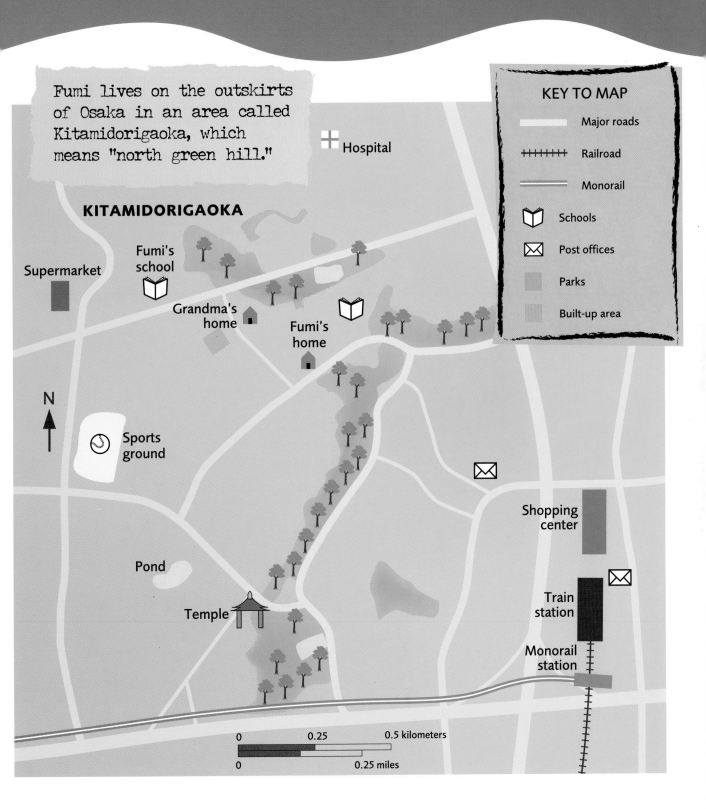

Fumi lives on the outskirts of Osaka in an area called Kitamidorigaoka, which means "north green hill."

Hospital

KITAMIDORIGAOKA

Supermarket

Fumi's school

Grandma's home

Fumi's home

KEY TO MAP

Major roads

Railroad

Monorail

Schools

Post offices

Parks

Built-up area

N

Sports ground

Pond

Temple

Shopping center

Train station

Monorail station

0   0.25   0.5 kilometers

0   0.25 miles

Osaka is an important port. It is in the center of Japan and is easy to reach by train, road, airplane, or ship. Electronic goods are made in Osaka and leave the country by ship.

Landscape and Weather

Japan is very mountainous. The country has many volcanoes and earthquakes are common. Most towns and cities are in the narrow, flat coastal areas. Osaka is known as the "city of water" because it has many rivers and is on the edge of a bay.

In the winter Fumi goes skiing in the mountains in Nagano, 300 miles (450 km) northeast of Osaka.

Most of Japan has a mild, humid climate. But because it stretches so far from north to south, it can be hot in the south and freezing in the north.

Fumi picks oranges in his uncle's orchard in southern Kyushu. Oranges grow well in the warm climate there.

Osaka's Climate

January
Temperature
43 °F
(6 °C)

Rainfall
4–5 in
(113 mm)

July
Temperature
82 °F
(28 °C)

Rainfall
5–6 in
(139 mm)

At Home

In Japan there is very little flat land on which to build houses. Like most Japanese people, Fumi's family lives in a small apartment in a large building. The family hangs out the washing on the balcony.

Fumi and Sota stand together outside their apartment building.

One of Fumi's chores is to wash the windows on the balcony.

In a small apartment everything needs to be tidy. Fumi does a lot of chores around the house. Sometimes he does the vacuuming and hangs out the washing. He also helps his mom with the shopping and cooking.

Space has to be used carefully in a small apartment. The washing machine and dryer are stacked up in the bathroom.

Fumi's house has the very latest technology. His family owns two televisions, two computers, a dishwasher, a microwave, and several stereos.

Fumi loves playing video games with his friends.

Fumi has his own bedroom. He does his homework at his desk just before he goes to bed.

Sunday, March 10

7-1-14-564
Kitamidorigaoka
Osaka 560-0001
Japan

Hi Nicky!

Have I told you about our special room? Although we have lots of modern things, we keep one room in the old Japanese style. There is no furniture and we sit on cushions. The floor is covered with straw mats called *tatami*. We always take off our shoes or slippers before we go into this room.

What's your home like?

From
Fumi

When friends stay over, we sleep in our traditional room on mattresses on the floor called *futons*.

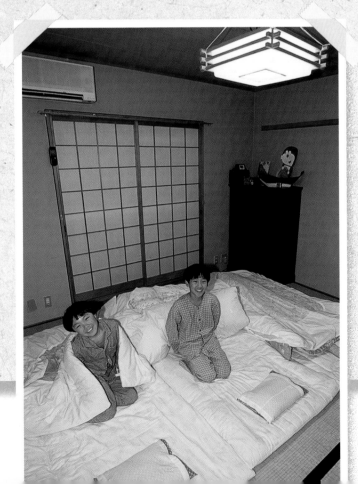

Food and Mealtimes

Fumi helps his mom carry
the shopping back from
the supermarket.

Fumi gets up at 7:30 A.M. For breakfast he usually has
egg and toast, fruit, vegetable juice, and a cup of tea.
On schooldays he has his lunch at school. At home,
lunch and dinner usually include rice or noodles.

Fumi eats lunch
in his classroom
with his friends.

Fumi's mom buys all the family's food at the supermarket. Fumi's family likes lots of different kinds of food, which they usually eat with chopsticks. Fumi's favorite foods are *sushi*, curry, and Western and Japanese-style pizza!

Fumi's family has a traditional Japanese meal of *sashimi*, which is raw fish.

Rice balls (*onigiri*) are usually eaten cold and are perfect for picnics.

Traditional Japanese food is very healthy. It is based on rice, fish, and vegetables. *Sushi* is very popular. *Sushi* is made from sticky rice topped with, or wrapped around different kinds of fish or omelet.

Fumi's family enjoys eating out together. This is a fast-food tent at a festival.

Friday, May 31

7-1-14-564
Kitamidorigaoka
Osaka 560-0001
Japan.

Ossu Nicky!

Here's that *sushi* recipe you asked for.

    You will need: 1 cup of short-grained rice, 1 cup water, 4 tablespoons rice vinegar, 1 tablespoon sugar, a small packet of smoked salmon, strips of cucumber, sheets of dried seaweed (you can buy this from a Japanese food shop).

1. Boil the rice in a saucepan until the water has gone.
2. Mix in the vinegar and sugar and leave to cool down.
3. Spread 2 tablespoons of rice on a sheet of dried seaweed.
4. Put a thin strip of salmon and cucumber on top and roll the seaweed round the filling to make an oblong.
5. Moisten the edge of the seaweed to make it stick, and slice into bite-sized pieces.

Try it dipped in soya sauce — it's delicious!

From
Fumi

Here I am rolling the *sushi* into an oblong.

School Day

Fumi goes to the primary school near his home.
Children at Fumi's school do not wear uniforms,
but they do have to wear the same gym clothes.

Fumi usually walks to
school with his friends.

School starts at 8:25 A.M. and finishes at 3:30 P.M. Fumi's favorite subjects are sports and science. He also studies Japanese, math, music, crafts, cooking, and sewing.

The principal leads morning assembly in the school playground.

This is Fumi's classroom. There are 35 children in his class.

Fumi's mom has been teaching him English since he was 6 years old. He will have English lessons at school when he is 12.

Japanese writing is made up of little pictures, called characters. There are more than 7,000 of them. Fumi has to learn more than 1,000 characters at primary school.

Children serving lunch wear masks so that they do not breathe germs on the food.

Fumi and his classmates have to clean their own classrooms, the toilets, and the playground. Everyone takes turns to serve school lunch.

Friday, September 27

7-1-14-564
Kitamidorigaoka
Osaka 560-0001
Japan

Dear Nicky,

I'm glad you did well on your Japan project. Today was my favorite day of the year — school sports day. Some of my friends put on a gymnastics display and some ran races. I took part in the tug of war — it was great fun!

We love sports in Japan. On the second Monday of October we have a national sports day — it's a public holiday. What's your favorite sport?

From

Fumi

Here's my team in the tug of war. We won the competition!

Off to Work

Fumi's mom is a high school teacher. She works part-time so she can look after the children when they come home from school. Fumi's dad is a photographer. His work takes him all over the world.

Fumi's mom sometimes gives extra lessons at her home to older students studying for exams.

In Japan, many people travel long distances by train every day to get to work.

These people are making electronic ticket barriers for Japan's train stations.

In Japan, many people work in stores and offices, or in the electronics industry. In Osaka there are lots of jobs in factories making cars and electronic equipment such as hi-fis and televisions.

Free Time

Fumi's dad is often away from home, so the family likes doing things together when they can. In the summer vacation they go swimming, fishing, and camping together. In the winter they like skiing.

Fumi playing *shogi* with his friend. This is a Japanese version of chess.

Fumi's sister helps him practice the piano.

Fumi has baseball practice on Saturdays and games almost every Sunday.

The Japanese love sports. Traditional sports such as judo and *sumo* wrestling are still popular, and many people are interested in soccer, baseball, and basketball.

Religion and Festivals

Buddhists wash their hands before they enter a temple. They use special cups outside.

Like many Japanese people, Fumi and his family are Buddhists. Shinto is the other main religion in Japan.

In November there is a special festival called *Shichigosan*. This is when parents give thanks to the gods for the health of their children. Some children wear kimonos (traditional Japanese clothes).

Shichigosan means the ages of the children taking part — seven (*shichi*), five (*go*), and three (*san*).

Friday, November 7

7-1-14-564
Kitamidorigaoka
Osaka 560-0001
Japan

Dear Nicky,

You wanted to know if we have any special festivals. We have lots! One special festival is *Obon* week, which is usually in July or August. We believe that the spirits of our ancestors visit us during this time. We visit our ancestors' graves and hang lanterns there. There are also special ceremonies at the temple. Then we float the lanterns on the river to guide the spirits home. It is really beautiful!

Sayonara
(This means goodbye.)

Fumi

During *Obon*, we had a special meal for my grandfather at the Buddhist temple.

Fact File

Capital City: The capital of Japan is Tokyo. It has a population of eight million.

Other Major Cities: Yokohama, Osaka, Nagoya, Sapporo, Kobe, and Kyoto.

Size: 115,300 square miles (378,000 km^2.)

Population: 126.5 million.

Language: Japanese.

Flag: The Japanese flag is known as the *Hinomaru*. The red circle is the rising sun. Japan is sometimes called the "Land of the Rising Sun."

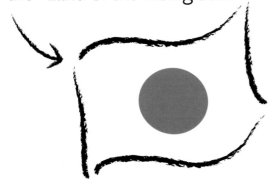

Main Religions: Most people in Japan follow Buddhism or Shinto.

Currency: The Japanese currency is known as the yen.

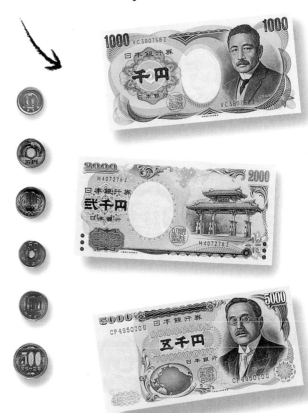

Highest Mountain: Mount Fuji 12,385 feet (3,776 m). Mount Fuji is a volcano. It last erupted in 1707.

Longest River: The longest river is the Shinano, 228 miles (367 km).

Main Industries: Japan exports cars, computers, and electronic equipment all over the world.

Earthquakes: Japan has about 1,000 small earthquakes each year. Sometimes there is a major one. The last major earthquake happened in Kobe, in 1995. All Japanese children learn what to do if there is an earthquake while they are at school. They must get under their desks and hold on to the legs of the desk until the earthquake has stopped.

Volcanoes: Japan has 83 active volcanoes, some of which may have several eruptions every year.

Royal Family: Japan's royal family can trace its ancestors back over 2,500 years. The current emperor, Emperor Akihito, calls his reign "*Heisei*", which means "the achievement of complete peace." The chrysanthemum is the symbol of the royal family.

Stamps: Japanese stamps show important buildings, art, birds, and animals of Japan. Some celebrate historical events.

Bullet Trains: The bullet train, or *shinkansen*, is one of the fastest trains in the world. It has a top speed of 200 miles (300 km) per hour.

Glossary

ancestors Family members that have died.

balcony A platform outside a window, usually with railings.

earthquake A violent shaking of the Earth's surface. Earthquakes can cause a lot of damage.

futon A traditional Japanese bed, made from a cotton mattress on a wooden frame. It is rolled out at night and put away in the morning.

humid climate A warm and damp weather system.

judo A Japanese sport that is similar to wrestling.

Obon week A special festival during which Japanese people remember their ancestors.

port A place where ships can load and unload their cargoes.

sashimi A traditional Japanese meal made from small pieces of raw fish.

sumo wrestling One of the most popular Japanese sports. The wrestlers are very heavy and try to topple each other outside the wrestling circle.

sushi A Japanese dish made from flavored sticky rice wrapped around fish or omelet. *Sushi* can be made into balls or rolls.

tatami Thick straw mats that cover the floors of traditional Japanese rooms.

temple A place of worship.

Further Information

Information books:

Fisher, Teresa. *We Come from Japan*. London: Hodder & Stoughton, 2002.

Fisher, Teresa. *Food and Festivals: A Flavour of Japan*. Chicago: Raintree, 1999.

Foster, Leila Merrell. *Continents: Asia*. Chicago: Heinemann Library, 2001.

Harvey, Miles. *Look What Came from Japan*. London: Franklin Watts, 1999.

Haslam, Andrew and Doran, Clare. *Make It Work! Japan*. Minnetonka, MN, 2001.

Lansford, Lewis and Schwarz, Chris. *The Changing Face of Japan*. London: Hodder & Stoughton Children's Division, 2002.

Fiction:

Hirezaki, Eiho; translated by Ralph F. McCarthy. *Grandfather Cherry-Blossom*. Cary, NC, 2000.

Pirotta, Saviour. *Turtle Bay*. London: Frances Lincoln, 1998.

Web sites:

CIA World Factbook
www.cia.gov/cia/publications/factbook/
Facts and figures about Japan and other countries.

Japan Information Network
http://jin.jcic.or.jp/atlas/
A look at Japan's architecture, festivals, and nature by region.

Kidsweb Japan
www.jinjapan.org/kidsweb/
This website has lots of basic facts and figures about Japan.

Index